ENGLISH TOWN

FOR EVERYONE

BOOK
6

Contents

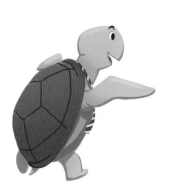

Theme Song

Hello Song

Hello, everyone.
Hello, teacher!
Hello, friends!

Let's have fun together.
We'll have a good time.

Are you ready to start?
We're ready!

Here we go!

Goodbye Song

Did you have fun?

It's time to say goodbye.
See you next time!
See you next time!

Did you enjoy the class?
Yes! We had a fun time!
Yes! We had a fun time!

See you later! See you later!
Goodbye. Goodbye.

Bye! Bye!

Lesson 1

It's an Action Movie

Let's Talk

A. Look, listen, and repeat.

Look! There's a new movie showing.

Really?

What kind of movie is it?

It's an action movie.

I'm crazy about action movies.

Let's go and see it.

Okay.

Movie Theater 100 m

ACT IT OUT

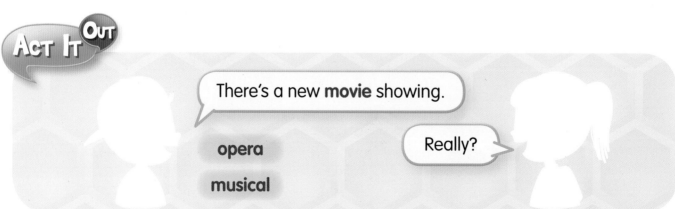

There's a new **movie** showing.

opera

musical

Really?

B. Listen and repeat.

It's an **action** movie.

①
action

②
horror

③
romantic

④
SF

What kind of movie is it?
– It's a(an) _____ movie.

C. Listen, point, and say.

① SF

② HORROR

③ ACTION

④ ROMANTIC

Let's Learn

A. Listen and chant.

Look! There's a new movie showing.

Really? Really? A new movie?

What kind of movie is it?

SF, SF, it's an SF movie.

Look! There's a new movie showing.

Really? Really? A new movie?

What kind of movie is it?

Horror, horror, it's a horror movie.

B. Read, look, and match.

① A: What kind of movie is it?

B: It's a horror movie.

② A: What kind of movie is it?

B: It's an action movie.

③ A: What kind of movie is it?

B: It's a romantic movie.

WEDDING

e-learning

A: What kind of movie is it?
B: It's **a fantasy** movie.

C. Match. Ask and answer.

 ①

 fantasy

romantic

 ④

 ②

comedy

action

⑤

③

horror

SF

⑥

A: What kind of movie is it?
B: It's **an action** movie.

D. Play the "Word Strip Bingo."

- Write five words from the word list and play the game.

word list   fantasy   romantic   action   comedy   horror   SF

Lesson 1 · **9**

Lesson 2

Let's Help Her

Let's Talk

A. Look, listen, and repeat.

That girl looks lost.

Oh! She's coming this way.

Let's help her.

Is there a movie theater near here?

We're going there. Come with us.

Okay. Thank you.

Yes, there's one on Pine Street.

ACT IT OUT

That girl looks **lost**.

sick

worried

Let's help her.

B. Listen and repeat.

Is there **an** animal clinic near here?

①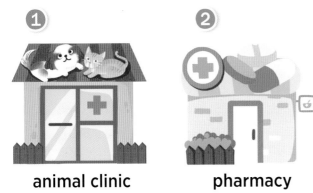

animal clinic

② pharmacy

③ sports center

④ stationery store

C. Listen, point, and say.

Is there a(an) _____ near here?
– Yes, there's one on _____ Street.

Let's Learn

A. Listen and chant.

Look! Look! That girl looks dizzy.

Help, help. Let's help her.

Is there a pharmacy near here?

Yes, there's one on Rosemary Street.

Look! Look! That girl looks lost.

Help, help. Let's help her.

Is there a sports center near here?

Yes, there's one on Pine Street.

B. Listen, look, and match.

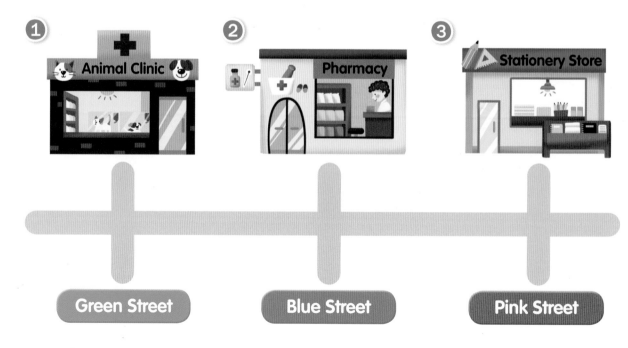

① Animal Clinic ② Pharmacy ③ Stationery Store

Green Street   Blue Street   Pink Street

A: Is there **an aquarium** near here?
B: Yes, there's one on **Blue** Street.

C. Ask, answer, and check.

① aquarium

BLUE | RED

② pharmacy

BLUE | RED

③ stationery store

BLUE | RED

④ sports center

BLUE | RED

⑤ animal clinic

BLUE | RED

⑥ bus stop

BLUE | RED

A: Is there an aquarium near here?
B: Yes, there's one on Amy Street.

D. Play the "Ladder Game."

aquarium   pharmacy   animal clinic   bus stop

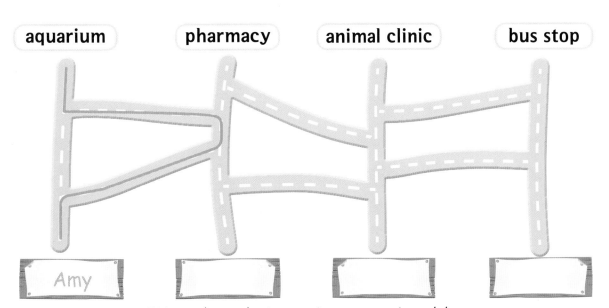

Amy

Write each member's name in your group in each box.

Welcome to Hawaii

A. Look, listen, and repeat.

B. Listen again and write the number in.

1 We're crazy about SF movies.

2 What kind of movie is it?

3 Walk up this street and turn left.

4 Excuse me. Is there a bus stop near here?

14

Bibble Paula Didi

C. Read and circle True or False.

1. Paula doesn't know Didi.   True   False
2. Bibble and Paula like SF movies. True   False
3. They decided to see the movie.   True   False
4. The bus stop is on Park Road.   True   False

D. Do a role-play.

Let's Play

A. Listen and sing.

What Kind of Movie Is It?

Is there a theater near here?
Yes, there's one on Red Street.
What kind of movie is it?
It is an action movie.

Is there a theater near here?
Yes, there's one on Blue Street.
What kind of movie is it?
It is a comedy movie.

B. Play a board game.

A: Is there a sports center near here?
B: Yes, there's one on Blue Street.

A: What kind of movie is it?
B: It's an action movie.

Reading Time

e-learning

Nicknames of Hawaii

Hawaii is called the **"Aloha State."**
"Aloha" means "Hello" and "Goodbye"
in Hawaiian words.
It means kindness and harmony, too.

Hawaii is called the **"Big Island."**
There is an active volcano, Kilauea.
It is on Crater Rim Drive.
The lava from the volcano makes new land.

Hawaii is called the **"Rainbow State."**
People can easily see rainbows in Hawaii.
Sometimes double rainbows appear.

CHECK IT OUT

1. What is the meaning of "Aloha"?

2. Why is Hawaii called the "Rainbow State"?

Lesson 4 Enjoy the Movie

Let's Talk

A. Look, listen, and repeat.

Let's get some soda and popcorn.

Good.

Our seats are in the fifth row.

You're not allowed to take pictures in here.

Enjoy the movie.

You, too.

Oh, sorry.

ACT IT OUT

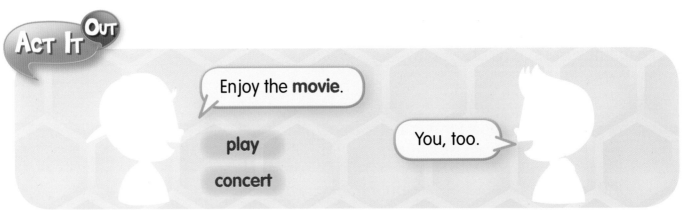

Enjoy the **movie**.

play

concert

You, too.

B. Listen and repeat.

You're not allowed to **bring your pet** in here.

bring your pet

copy the book

eat or drink

speak loudly

C. Listen, point, and say.

You're not allowed to _____ in here.
– Oh, sorry.

Let's Learn

A. Listen and chant.

Let's go to the art gallery, the art gallery.

You're not allowed to eat or drink in here.

Sorry, sorry, I didn't know that.

Enjoy your time. Enjoy your time.

Let's go to the library, the library.

You're not allowed to speak loudly in here.

Sorry, sorry, I didn't know that.

Study hard! Study hard!

B. Read, look, and match.

1. You're not allowed to eat or drink. •

2. You're not allowed to copy the book. •

3. You're not allowed to bring your pet. •

4. You're not allowed to speak loudly. •

C. Match and talk.

A: You're not allowed to **feed the animals**.
B: Oh, sorry.

①

_____ the animals

②

_____ or drink

③

_____ loudly

take   feed   bring   eat   copy   speak

④

_____ pictures

⑤

_____ your pet

⑥

_____ the book

D. Write and talk.

A: You're not allowed to speak loudly
in the library.
B: Oh, sorry.

	Restaurant	Library	Zoo
		• speak loudly	

Lesson 5

It Was Interesting

Let's Talk

A. Look, listen, and repeat.

- It was interesting.
- No, it was boring.
- I like romantic movies.
- Did you enjoy the movie?
- Yeah, I want to be a hero like him.
- HA HA HA
- Yes, it was very exciting.
- Same here.

I want to be a **hero** like him.

cook

teacher

Same here.

B. Listen and repeat.

It was boring .

①
boring

②
fantastic

③
terrible

④
touching

C. Listen, point, and say.

Did you enjoy the play?
– Yes(No), it was _____.

① boring

② touching

③ terrible

④ fantastic

Let's Learn

A. Listen and chant.

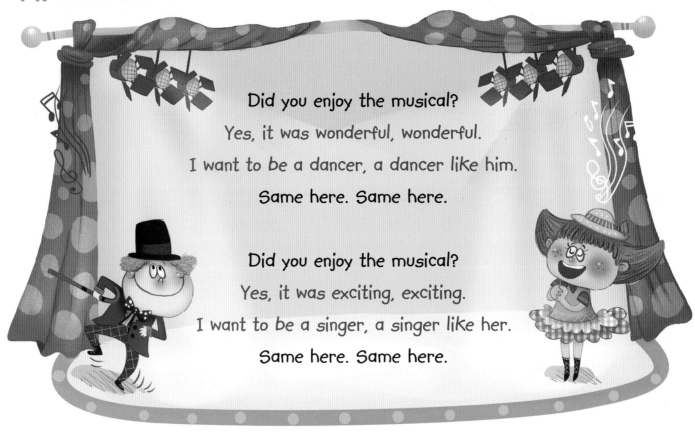

Did you enjoy the musical?
Yes, it was wonderful, wonderful.
I want to be a dancer, a dancer like him.
Same here. Same here.

Did you enjoy the musical?
Yes, it was exciting, exciting.
I want to be a singer, a singer like her.
Same here. Same here.

B. Listen, look, and number.

❶

❷

❸

❹

A: Did you enjoy the movie?
B: Yes (No), it was **funny**.

C. Ask, answer, and check.

1 funny
☺ ☹

2 fantastic
☺ ☹

3 boring
☺ ☹

4 scary
☺ ☹

5 terrible
☺ ☹

6 touching
☺ ☹

A: Did you enjoy the movie?
B: Yes, it was fantastic.

D. Ask and answer. Then write.

movie
☑ Yes _fantastic_
☐ No _____

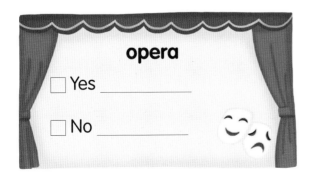

opera
☐ Yes _____
☐ No _____

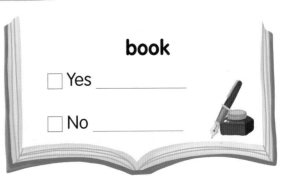

book
☐ Yes _____
☐ No _____

Lesson 5 · 25

Lesson 6 — At the Movie Theater

A. Look, listen and repeat.

B. Listen again and write the number in.

1. You're not allowed to take pictures here.
2. 5A, 5B, and 5C.
3. I want to be an astronaut like her.
4. Did you enjoy the movie?

Bibble Paula Didi

Sorry, I didn't know that.

Same here.

Yes, it was fantastic.

C. Read and circle True or False.

1. They should sit in 15A, 15B, and 15C.   True   False

2. Paula took Bibble's picture.   True   False

3. Paula wants to be an astronaut.   True   False

4. Bibble didn't enjoy the movie.   True   False

D. Do a role-play.

A. Listen and sing.

It's Party Time

Party, party, it's party time.
You're not allowed to be sad.
Did you enjoy the party?
Yes, it was cool.

Lunch, lunch, it's lunch time.
You're not allowed to shout.
Did you enjoy the lunch?
Yes, it was great.

B. Play a board game.

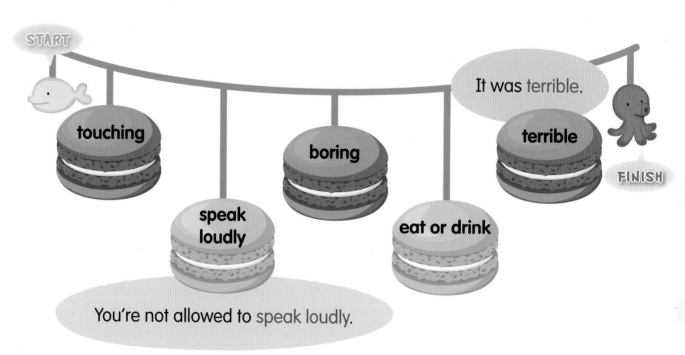

START

touching

speak loudly

boring

eat or drink

It was terrible.

terrible

FINISH

You're not allowed to speak loudly.

e-learning

World Records for Movies

Where is the largest IMAX movie screen?
It's in Sydney, Australia.
It's 35.72m wide and 29.57m high.
It's as tall as a seven-story building.

What do you know about India? Curry?
India makes the most movies a year.
Over 1,000 movies are made every year in India.
That's almost double the number of movies made in Hollywood.

This is 455m long. Can you recognize what it is?
It's a red carpet for the movie première of *Harry Potter*.
The carpet stretched from Trafalgar Square to Leicester Square in London, the United Kingdom, on 7 July 2011.
It's the longest red carpet for a movie première.

CHECK IT OUT

1. How big is the largest IMAX movie screen?
2. Which country makes the most movies?

Lesson 7

Here Is Your Bag

Let's Talk

A. Look, listen, and repeat.

Get him!

Could you give me the ball?

Okay.

Go Bob! You can do it!

Here is your bag.

Thank you.

ACT IT OUT

Here is your **bag**.

phone

umbrella

Thank you.

B. Listen and repeat.

Could you plant the flower ?

① plant the flower

② sow the seeds

③ trim the tree

④ water the lawn

C. Listen, point, and say.

Could you _____ ?
– Okay.

Let's Learn

A. Listen and chant.

Could you, could you trim the tree?

Okay. Okay. Okay.

Here are the scissors, the scissors.

Thank you. Thank you.

Could you, could you sow the seeds?

Okay. Okay. Okay.

Here are the seeds, the seeds.

Thank you. Thank you.

B. Look, read, and choose.

①

A: Could you ⓐ trim / ⓑ water the tree?

B: Okay.

②

A: Could you plant the ⓐ tree / ⓑ flower ?

B: Okay.

③

A: Could you ⓐ sow / ⓑ mow the seeds?

B: Okay.

A: Could you **dig a hole**?
B: Okay.

C. Match. Ask and answer.

① _____ a hole

② _____ the flower

③ _____ the lawn

mow　dig　trim　plant　sow　water

④ _____ the tree

⑤ _____ the lawn

⑥ _____ the seeds

D. Play the "Bingo!": Write. Ask and answer.

B I N G O

A: Could you dig a hole?
B: Okay.

To Do in Gardening

• dig a hole
• plant the flower
• water the lawn
• trim the tree
• mow the lawn
• sow the seeds

It's a Little Bit Salty

Let's Talk

A. Look, listen, and repeat.

Mmm.... The pizzas smell good.

Let's buy one.

Okay.

How does it taste?

Can I have another pizza?

Sure. You eat a lot!

It's a little bit salty, but it's okay.

ACT IT OUT

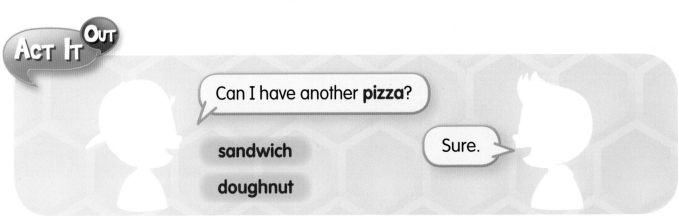

Can I have another **pizza**?

sandwich

doughnut

Sure.

B. Listen and repeat.

It's a little bit bitter .

bitter

salty

sour

spicy

C. Listen, point, and say.

How does it taste?
– It's a little bit _____.

Let's Learn

A. Listen and chant.

Kiwi juice, kiwi juice. How does it taste?

It's a little bit sour, but it's okay.

Can I have some more juice?

Sure, sure, you can.

Pizza, pizza. How does it taste?

It's a little bit salty, but it's okay.

Can I have some more pizza?

Sorry, sorry, you can't.

B. Listen, look, and check.

 ①

 ②

③

 ④

A: How does it taste?
B: It's a little bit **greasy**.

C. Check. Ask and answer.

① ☐ sour
☐ greasy

② ☐ bitter
☐ sweet

③ ☐ spicy
☐ greasy

④ ☐ sour
☐ spicy

⑤ ☐ salty
☐ sweet

⑥ ☐ sour
☐ sweet

D. Draw. Then ask and answer.

A: How does it taste?
B: It's a little bit salty.

Taste: _____

Taste: _____

Lesson 9 — At a Hawaiian Restaurant

A. Look, listen, and repeat.

B. Listen again and write the number in.

1. This restaurant is the best in Hawaii. Let's go in.
2. Sure. Here you are.
3. May I take your order?
4. It's not salty enough, but it's okay.

Bibble   Paula   Didi   Tutu

C. Read and circle True or False.

1. They are at a Chinese restaurant.   True   False

2. The food was too sweet for Paula.   True   False

3. Paula asked Tutu for salt.   True   False

4. Paula is full.   True   False

D. Do a role-play.

A. Listen and sing.

How Does It Taste?

Could you pass me the sugar?

Okay. Here you are.

How does it taste?

It's a little bit sweet, but it's okay.

Could you pass me the salt?

Okay. Here you are.

How does it taste?

It's a little bit salty, but it's okay.

B. Play a board game.

It's a little bit spicy.

Could you sow the seeds?

e-learning

3 Foods to Eat for Health

Olive Oil
Olive oil is a little bit bitter, but it is good for us.
It helps keep our skin healthy and prevents cavities.
It also protects our bodies against aging.

Yogurt
Greek yogurt is a little bit sour, but it is good for your bones.
It also helps your body to fight disease.
Greek people put some yogurt in hamburgers.
They're healthy and delicious.

Gimchi
Gimchi is a little bit spicy, but it is good for your health.
It has a lot of vitamin A, B, and C.
Korean people like it.

CHECK IT OUT

1. Which food is good for our bones?

2. Which food has a lot of vitamins?

Lesson 10

Assessment Test 1

A. Look, listen, and check.

①  a. ☐
    b. ☐

②  a. ☐
    b. ☐

③  a. ☐
    b. ☐

④  a. ☐
    b. ☐

⑤  a. ☐
    b. ☐

⑥  a. ☐
    b. ☐

B. Listen and choose the answer.

1. What kind of movie is showing?

ⓐ An SF movie is showing.

ⓑ An action movie is showing.

2. Where can Jenny eat food?

ⓐ She can eat food in the library.

ⓑ She can eat food in the cafeteria.

A. Look and practice the dialog.

❶

A How does it taste?
B It's a little bit spicy.

❷

A Did you enjoy the movie?
B Yes, it was fantastic.

❸

A Could you plant the flower?
B Okay.

❹

A Is there an aquarium near here?
B Yes, there's one on Red Street.

B. Number the sentences in order and practice the dialog.

( ) Sorry, I didn't know that.

(1) What are you doing?

( ) You're not allowed to copy the book.

( ) I'm copying a book.

A. Read and match.

1. Can I have another pizza? •

2. Here is your bag. •

3. How does it taste? •

4. There's a new movie showing. •

5. The girl looks lost. •

6. I want to be a hero like him. •

• **a.** Thank you.

• **b.** Let's help her.

• **c.** Really?

• **d.** Sure, you can.

• **e.** Same here.

• **f.** It's a little bitter.

B. Read and check True or False.

(A) Paula Take my picture.
Bibble Okay. Say cheese!
Staff   You're not allowed to take pictures in the theater.
Paula Sorry, I didn't know that.

(B) Didi   How does the food taste?
Paula It's not salty enough, but it's okay. Could you pass me the salt?
Tutu   Sure. Here you are.

1. Paula can't take her picture in the theater.   True ☐   False ☐

2. The food is too salty for Paula.   True ☐   False ☐

3. Tutu gave the salt to Paula.   True ☐   False ☐

4. Writing

e-learning

> sour   terrible   romantic   stationery store
> animal clinic   trim the tree   speak loudly   sow the seeds

A. Choose and write.

①

_____

②

_____

③

_____

④

_____

⑤

_____

⑥

_____

⑦

_____

⑧

_____

B. Unscramble the words.

1. **A** How does it taste?

   B _____
   (it's / okay / It's / sweet, / a little bit / but / .)

2. **A** Did you enjoy the movie?

   B _____
   (was / it / exciting / Yes, / very / .)

3. **A** _____
   (a movie theater / here / Is / near / there / ?)

   B Yes, there's one on Pine Street.

Lesson 11

What's Up?

Let's Talk

A. Look, listen, and repeat.

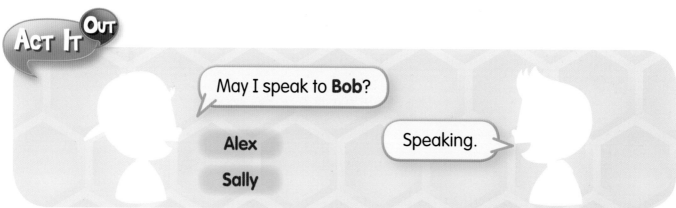

ACT IT OUT

B. Listen and repeat.

I'm calling to ask for advice .

ask for advice

ask for help

say sorry

say thank you

C. Listen, point, and say.

What's up?
– I'm calling to _____ .

Let's Learn

A. Listen and chant.

Hello? Hello? This is Tommy.

May I speak to Jenny?

Speaking, speaking. What's up?

I'm calling to ask for advice, ask for advice.

Hello? Hello? This is Kate.

May I speak to Paul?

Speaking, speaking. What's up?

I'm calling to say thank you, say thank you.

B. Listen, look, and match.

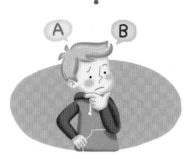

Thank you.

A: What's up?
B: I'm calling to **say thank you**.

C. Roll the dice. Then ask and answer.

① say thank you

② ask for help

③ say goodbye

④ invite you to dinner

⑤ say sorry

⑥ ask for advice

D. Ask and answer. Then write.

A: What's up, Jenny?
B: I'm calling to say thank you.

from: Jenny
To say thank you.

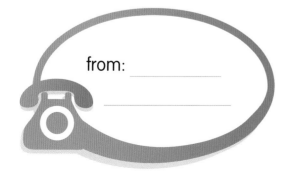

from: _____
_____

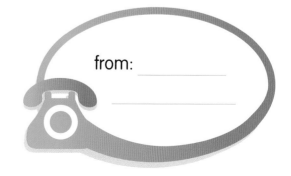

from: _____
_____

Lesson 12

Can You Take Me to Thomas' Lab?

Let's Talk

A. Look, listen, and repeat.

Mom, can you take me to Thomas' Lab?

Sure.

The traffic is heavy.

Mom, let me off here.

Okay.

Call me when you get there.

Okay, I will.

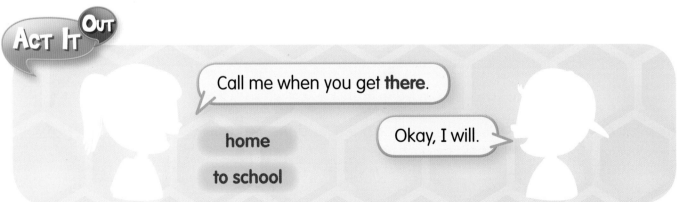

Call me when you get **there**.

home

to school

Okay, I will.

B. Listen and repeat.

Can you take me to the **bookstore** ?

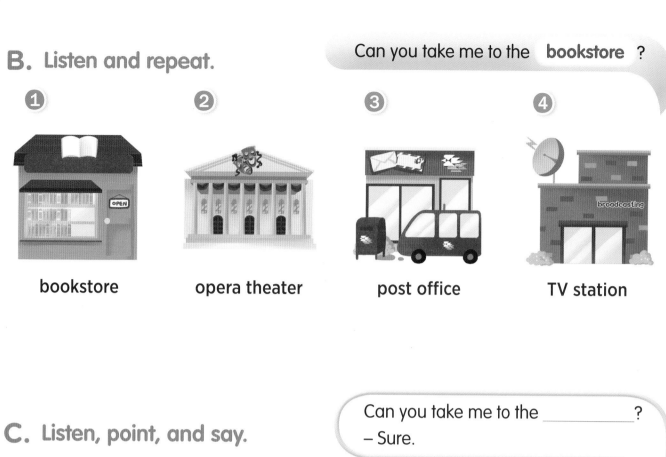

① bookstore

② opera theater

③ post office

④ TV station

C. Listen, point, and say.

Can you take me to the _____ ?
– Sure.

① TV STATION
② BOOKSTORE
③ POST OFFICE
④ OPERA THEATER

Let's Learn

A. Listen and chant.

Can you take me to the post office?

Sure, sure. No problem.

Tell me, tell me when you get there.

Okay, okay, I will.

Can you take me to the aquarium?

Sure, sure. No problem.

Tell me, tell me when you get there.

Okay, okay, I will.

B. Read, look, and choose.

1 Can you take me to the airport?

ⓐ 　　ⓑ

2 Can you take me to the bookstore?

ⓐ 　　ⓑ

3 Can you take me to the TV station?

ⓐ 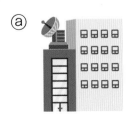　　ⓑ

4 Can you take me to the post office?

ⓐ 　　ⓑ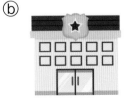

A: Can you take me to the **opera theater**?

B: Sure.

C. Choose three places. Ask and answer.

1 opera theater ☐

2 post office ☐

3 bookstore ☐

4 airport ☐

5 TV station ☐

6 hospital ☐

D. Do "Rock-Paper-Scissors": Ask, answer, and color.

Can you take me to the airport?

Sure, I can.

Sorry, I can't.

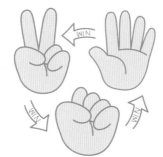

Places	airport	post office	bookstore	opera theater	TV station	hospital
Points						

Lesson 13 An Invitation to a Party

A. Look, listen, and repeat.

B. Listen again and write the number in.

1. What's up?
2. Thank you.
3. Can you take me to Tutu's house?
4. Okay! I'm so excited.

54

C. **Read and circle True or False.**

1. Bibble called Tutu.   True   False
2. Tutu invited Bibble to her party.   True   False
3. Didi can drive.   True   False
4. Bibble will go to the party with Didi.   True   False

D. **Do a role-play.**

A. Listen and sing.

What's Up?

Ring - ring - ring. What's up?
I'm calling to ask for help.
Can you take me to the sea?
Sure, I can. Let's go.

Ring - ring - ring. What's up?
I'm calling to ask for help.
Can you take me to the mountain?
Sure, I can. Let's go.

B. Play a board game.

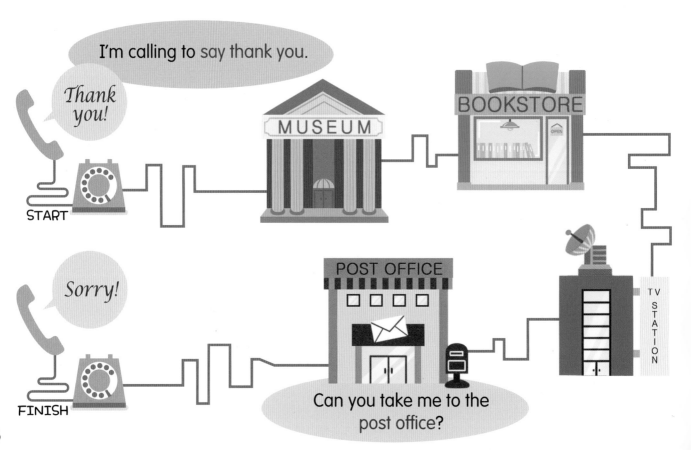

I'm calling to say thank you.

Thank you!

MUSEUM

BOOKSTORE

START

Sorry!

POST OFFICE

TV STATION

FINISH

Can you take me to the post office?

e-learning

Surviving on a Desert Island

If you are alone on an island, what will you do?
Don't be scared. Just do these things in order.

1. Find water you can drink.
2. Build a shelter.
3. Build a fire.
4. Make a rescue signal fire.
5. Find some food you can eat.

If you see a ship or a plane, light your
rescue signal fire. Then wave your arms
and jump up and down.
Shout HELP! Can you take me home?

1. What is the most important thing to do first?
2. What should you do if you see a ship or a plane?

Lesson 14

I Have Something to Show You

Let's Talk

A. Look, listen, and repeat.

Who's there?

It's me.

Sorry. I'm late because of the heavy traffic.

That's okay.

These are for you.

Umm, it's good.

Look! I have something to show you.

I can't wait to see it.

I have something to **show** you.

tell / hear

give / get

I can't wait to **see** it.

B. Listen and repeat.

 I'm late because of **a car accident** .

a car accident

a flat tire

the heavy snow

the roadwork

C. Listen, point, and say.

I'm late because of _____.
– That's okay.

Let's Learn

A. Listen and chant.

Who's there? Who's there?
It's me. I have something to tell you.
I'm late because of a car accident.
That's okay. That's okay.

Who's there? Who's there?
It's me. I have something to tell you.
I'm late because of the heavy snow.
That's okay. That's okay.

B. Look, read, and check.

1

2

3

1
- [ ] I'm late because of the roadwork.
- [ ] I'm late because of a traffic jam.

2
- [ ] I'm late because of a car accident.
- [ ] I'm late because of a flat tire.

3
- [ ] I'm late because of the heavy rain.
- [ ] I'm late because of the heavy snow.

A: I'm late because of **the roadwork**.
B: That's okay.

C. Match and talk.

1

2

3

the roadwork

a car accident

the heavy rain

a traffic jam

a flat tire

the heavy snow

4

5

6

D. Play the "Sentence Relay Game."

I'm late because of a traffic jam.

Tom is late because of a traffic jam.
I'm late because of a car accident.

Tom is late .... Jane is late ....
I'm late because of ....

Tom is .... Jane is .... Anne is ....
I'm late because of ....

Lesson 15 My Key Is Missing

Let's Talk

A. Look, listen, and repeat.

Wow! What's that?

It's my new invention.

What is it? I'm so excited.

Me, too.

Uh-oh... my key is missing.

Go on, open the box.

Really? Let's look for it together.

ACT IT OUT

I'm so **excited**.

tired

surprised

Me, too.

B. Listen and repeat.

My backpack is missing.

① backpack

② cell phone

③ key

④ wallet

C. Listen, point, and say.

My _____ is missing.
– Let's look for it together.

Let's Learn

A. Listen and chant.

Oh, no! Oh, no! My wallet is missing.

Really? Really? Let's look for it together.

I'm sad. I'm so sad.

Me, too. Me, too.

Oh, no! Oh, no! My backpack is missing.

Really? Really? Let's look for it together.

I'm worried. I'm so worried.

Me, too. Me, too.

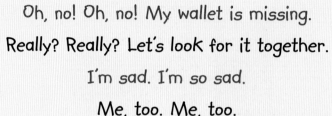

B. Listen, look, and number.

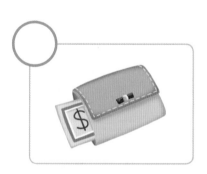

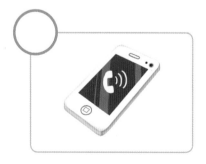

64

A: My **key** is missing.
B: Let's look for it together.

C. Match a puzzle and talk.

①  ② ③  ④ ⑤ ⑥

wallet   key   backpack   necklace   cell phone   helmet

D. Find and color the hidden items.

A: My backpack is missing.
B: Let's look for it together.

Lesson 16 · A Gift for Tutu

A. Look, listen, and repeat.

B. Listen again and write the number in.

1. I agree.

2. How about buying a gift for Tutu?

3. The parking ticket is missing.

4. That's okay. How beautiful!

66

C. Read and circle True or False.

1. Paula wanted to buy a gift for Tutu.   True   False

2. Bibble doesn't want to see Tutu.   True   False

3. Didi lost a movie ticket.   True   False

4. Tutu is upset because Bibble is late.   True   False

D. Do a role-play.

A. Listen and sing.

I'm Late Today

Hi, sorry, sorry, I'm late today.
I'm late because of the rain.
Oh, no! My umbrella is missing.
Let's look for it together.

Hi, sorry, sorry, I'm late today.
I'm late because of the snow.
Oh, no! My gloves are missing.
Let's look for them together.

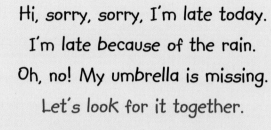

B. Play a board game.

START

My cell phone
is missing.

I'm late because
of a car accident.

Finish

e-learning

Tom's Diary: Candy Is Missing

Dear. Diary,

During lunch Mom called. She said, "I can't find Candy. She is missing." In the afternoon I couldn't study. I was thinking about Candy. Where is she? Did she run away?

After school I ran to my home. Where is Candy? I looked everywhere for her, but I couldn't find her. Then I went to my room and opened the closet.

Candy was there. She was very happy to see me. She jumped on me and licked my face.

1. Why did Tom's mom call Tom?

2. Where was Candy?

Lesson 17
I Smell Something Greasy

Let's Talk

A. Look, listen, and repeat.

I smell something greasy.

So do I.

Stella, is it you?

No, it isn't me.

It isn't me, either.

What's your new invention?

It's a robot cat, Rocat.

A robot cat? Hmm ....
Now, I got it.

ACT IT OUT

What's your new invention?

doctor

teacher

It's a robot **cat**.

70

B. Listen and repeat.

I hear something beeping .

①

hear / beeping

②

hear / crying

③

smell / burning

④

smell / rotten

C. Listen, point, and say.

I _____ something _____ .
– So do I.

Let's Learn

A. Listen and chant.

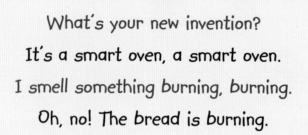

What's your new invention?
It's a smart oven, a smart oven.
I smell something burning, burning.
Oh, no! The bread is burning.

What's your new invention?
It's a robot bird, a robot bird.
I hear something crying, crying.
Oh, no! The bird is crying.

B. Look, read, and number.

① 　② 　③

_____ A: I smell something rotten.　　B: So do I.

_____ A: I smell something burning.　　B: So do I.

_____ A: I hear something beeping.　　B: So do I.

A: I **hear** something **breaking**.
B: So do I.

C. Match and talk.

1
hear...

breaking

rotten

4
smell...

2
hear...

crying

baking

5
smell...

3
hear...

beeping

burning

6
smell...

D. Write and talk.

- What do you hear and smell at home?

A: I hear my brother crying.
B: So do I.

Hear	Smell
• I hear my brother crying.	• I smell my mom cooking.

Lesson 18

What a Surprise!

Let's Talk

A. Look, listen, and repeat.

Rodog, give the key back to us.

Sorry, I don't like cats.

But Rodog, I made Rocat for you.

What a surprise!

I'm sure you're happy now, Rodog.

Yes, I am.

 ACT IT OUT

I made **Rocat** for you.

a sweater

dinner

What a surprise!

74

B. Listen and repeat.

I'm sure you're   brave .

brave   gentle   humorous   outgoing

C. Listen, point, and say.

I'm sure you're _____.
– Yes, I am.

Let's Learn

A. Listen and chant.

I did it for you, for you.
What a surprise! What a surprise!
I'm sure you're brave, brave.
Thank you. Thank you.

I made it for you, for you.
What a surprise! What a surprise!
I'm sure you're kind, kind.
Thank you. Thank you.

B. Listen, read, and match.

❶ Mike

❷ Anne

❸ June

❹ Sally

I'm sure you're gentle.

I'm sure you're outgoing.

I'm sure you're brave.

I'm sure you're humorous.

A: I'm sure you're **gentle**.
B: Yes, I am.

C. Go down the ladder. Then talk.

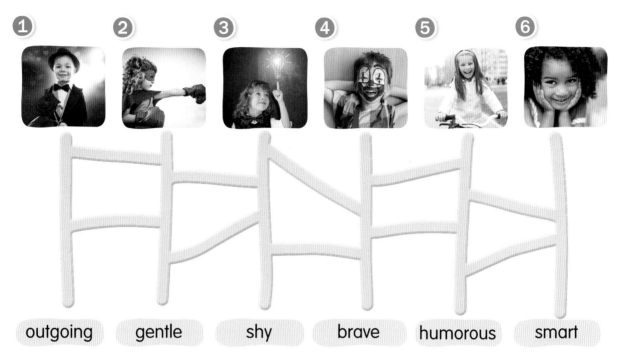

① ② ③ ④ ⑤ ⑥

outgoing　gentle　shy　brave　humorous　smart

D. Write and talk.

A: I'm sure Jenny is smart.
B: Yes, she is.

Jenny	smart

Lesson 19

A Party at Tutu's House

A. Look, listen, and repeat.

B. Listen again and write the number in.

1. Thank you for inviting us.

2. Have fun and enjoy the food.

3. Hold on, I smell something cooking.

4. Yes, I am. I'm starving.

Bibble Paula Didi Tutu

C. Read and circle True or False.

1. They are at Tutu's house.　　True　False
2. Bibble smelled something cooking.　　True　False
3. Bibble was not hungry.　　True　False
4. Tutu is having a barbecue party.　　True　False

D. Do a role-play.

Let's Play

A. Listen and sing.

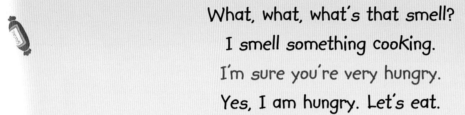

Smell and Hear

What, what, what's that smell?
I smell something cooking.
I'm sure you're very hungry.
Yes, I am hungry. Let's eat.

What, what, what's that sound?
I hear something coming.
I'm sure you're very nervous.
Yes, I am nervous. Let's run.

B. Play a board game.

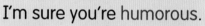
I'm sure you're humorous.

I smell something rotten.

Try again!

Personality Types

Here are three personality types: Which one are you?

TYPE 1 FUN-LOVING

Do you like surprise parties? I'm sure you are the Fun-loving type. Type 1 people love to meet people.

TYPE 2 HELPFUL

Do you like to help others? You are the helpful type. Type 2 people have a warm heart. They are kind and gentle.

TYPE 3 INDEPENDENT

Do you like competition like sports and games? You are the independent type. Type 3 people like to move fast and are very energetic.

1. Who likes to meet people?

2. Who likes to help others?

1. Listening

A. Look, listen, and check.

①
   a. ☐
   b. ☐

②
   a. ☐
   b. ☐

③
   a. ☐
   b. ☐

④
   a. ☐
   b. ☐

⑤
   a. ☐
   b. ☐

⑥
   a. ☐
   b. ☐

B. Listen and choose the answer.

1. Why is Stacy late?

   ⓐ She is late because of the roadwork.

   ⓑ She is late because of the heavy rain.

2. What is missing?

   ⓐ Amy's wallet is missing.

   ⓑ Amy's cell phone is missing.

A. Look and practice the dialog.

A I'm sure you're smart.

B Yes, I am.

A Can you take me to the airport?

B Sure.

A I smell something burning.

B So do I.

A What's up?

B I'm calling to invite you to dinner.

B. Number the sentences in order and practice the dialog.

(1) Who's there?

( ) That's okay.

( ) It's me.

( ) Sorry. I'm late because of the heavy traffic.

A. Read and match.

1. Call me when you get home. •

2. I have something to show you. •

3. I'm so tired. •

4. What's your new invention? •

5. I made dinner for you. •

6. May I speak to Jenny? •

• **a.** Speaking.

• **b.** What a surprise!

• **c.** Okay, I will.

• **d.** I can't wait to see it.

• **e.** Me, too.

• **f.** It's a robot cat.

B. Read and choose the answer.

(A) Bibble What's up?
Tutu   I'm calling to invite you and Paula to my party.

(B) Paula How about buying these flowers for Tutu?
Bibble Sounds great.

(C) Bibble These are for you.
Tutu   What beautiful flowers!

(D) Paula I smell something cooking here.
Tutu   We're having a barbecue party.

1. Tutu invited Bibble and Paula to her _____.
   ⓐ party   ⓑ concert

2. Paula and Bibble bought some _____ for Tutu.
   ⓐ flowers   ⓑ barbecue

3. Paula smells something _____.
   ⓐ burning   ⓑ cooking

4. Writing

e-learning

opera theater   ask for advice

beeping   rotten   backpack

humorous   post office   roadwork

A. Choose and write.

①

_____

②

_____

③

_____

④

_____

⑤

_____

⑥

_____

⑦

_____

⑧

_____

B. Unscramble the words.

1. A _____

(smell / greasy / something / I / .)

B So do I.

2. A _____

(you / Can / take / to / me / Thomas' Lab / ?)

B Sure.

3. A _____

(is / key / My / missing / .)

B Really? Let's look for it together.

Syllabus

Lesson	Topic	Language	Key Vocabulary
Lesson 1	It's an Action Movie	What kind of movie is it? - It's an action movie. There's a new movie showing. - Really?	action horror romantic SF
Lesson 2	Let's Help Her	Is there a movie theater near here? - Yes, there's one on Pine Street. That girl looks lost. - Let's help her.	animal clinic pharmacy sports center stationery store
Lesson 3	Welcome to Hawaii	Step Up 1 (Review Lessons 1-2) *Reading Time: Nicknames of Hawaii	
Lesson 4	Enjoy the Movie	You're not allowed to take pictures in here. - Oh, sorry. Enjoy the movie. - You, too.	bring your pet copy the book eat or drink speak loudly
Lesson 5	It Was Interesting	Did you enjoy the movie? - Yes, it was very exciting. I want to be a hero like him. - Same here.	boring fantastic terrible touching
Lesson 6	At the Movie Theater	Step Up 2 (Review Lessons 4-5) *Reading Time: World Records for Movies	
Lesson 7	Here Is Your Bag	Could you give me the ball? - Okay. Here is your bag. - Thank you.	plant the flower sow the seeds trim the tree water the lawn
Lesson 8	It's a Little Bit Salty	How does it taste? - It's a little bit salty, but it's okay. Can I have another pizza? - Sure.	bitter salty sour spicy
Lesson 9	At a Hawaiian Restaurant	Step Up 3 (Review Lessons 7-8) *Reading Time: 3 Foods to Eat for Health	
Lesson 10		**Assessment Test 1** (Review Lessons 1-9)	

Lesson	Topic	Language	Key Vocabulary
Lesson 11	What's Up?	What's up? - I'm calling to invite you to my lab. May I speak to Bob? - Speaking.	ask for advice ask for help say sorry say thank you
Lesson 12	Can You Take Me to Thomas' Lab?	Can you take me to Thomas' Lab? - Sure. Call me when you get there. - Okay, I will.	bookstore opera theater post office TV station
Lesson 13	An Invitation to a Party	Step Up 4 (Review Lessons 11-12) *Reading Time: Surviving on a Desert Island	
Lesson 14	I Have Something to Show You	I'm late because of the heavy traffic. - That's okay. I have something to show you. - I can't wait to see it.	a car accident a flat tire the heavy snow the roadwork
Lesson 15	My Key Is Missing	My key is missing. - Let's look for it together. I'm so excited. - Me, too.	backpack cell phone key wallet
Lesson 16	A Gift for Tutu	Step Up 5 (Review Lessons 14-15) *Reading Time: Tom's Diary: Candy Is Missing	
Lesson 17	I Smell Something Greasy	I smell something greasy. - So do I. What's your new invention? - It's a robot cat, Rocat.	hear / beeping hear / crying smell / burning smell / rotten
Lesson 18	What a Surprise!	I'm sure you're happy now, Rodog. - Yes, I am. I made Rocat for you. - What a surprise!	brave gentle humorous outgoing
Lesson 19	A Party at Tutu's House	Step Up 6 (Review Lessons 17-18) *Reading Time: Personality Types	
Lesson 20	Assessment Test 2 (Review Lessons 11-19)		

Flashcard List

	action		horror		romantic
	SF		animal clinic		pharmacy
	sports center		stationery store		bring your pet
	copy the book		eat or drink		speak loudly
	boring		fantastic		terrible
	touching		plant the flower		sow the seeds
	trim the tree		water the lawn		bitter
	salty		sour		spicy
	ask for advice		ask for help		say sorry
	say thank you		bookstore		opera theater
	post office		TV station		car accident
	flat tire		heavy snow		roadwork
	backpack		cell phone		key
	wallet		hear / beeping		hear / crying
	smell / burning		smell / rotten		brave
	gentle		humorous		outgoing

Lesson 1 It's an Action Movie

	Vocabulary	Meaning	Sentence
1	action*	액션	It's an action movie.
2	horror*	공포	It's a horror movie.
3	romantic*	낭만적인	It's a romantic movie.
4	SF*	공상 과학	It's an SF movie.
5	fantasy	판타지, 환상	It's a fantasy movie.
6	comedy	희극	It's a comedy movie.
7	movie	영화	There's a new movie showing.
8	opera	오페라	There's a new opera showing.
9	musical	뮤지컬	There's a new musical showing.
10	new	새로운	There's a new movie showing.
11	kind of	종류의	What kind of movie is it?
12	crazy about	~에 열광적인	I'm crazy about action movies.

Lesson 2 Let's Help Her

	Vocabulary	Meaning	Sentence
1	animal clinic*	동물 병원	Is there an animal clinic near here?
2	pharmacy*	약국	Is there a pharmacy near here?
3	sports center*	스포츠 센터	Is there a sports center near here?
4	stationery store*	문구점	Is there a stationery store near here?
5	aquarium	수족관	Is there an aquarium near here?
6	bus stop	버스 정류장	Is there a bus stop near here?
7	lost	길을 잃은	That girl looks lost.
8	sick	아픈	That girl looks sick.
9	worried	걱정되는	That girl looks worried.
10	help	돕다	Let's help her.
11	theater	극장	Is there a movie theater near here?
12	near	~의 가까이(에)	Is there a movie theater near here?

Lesson 5 It Was Interesting

	Vocabulary	Meaning	Sentence
1	boring*	따분한	No, it was boring.
2	fantastic*	환상적인	Yes, it was fantastic.
3	terrible*	끔찍한	No, it was terrible.
4	touching*	감동적인	Yes, it was touching.
5	funny	재미있는	Yes, it was funny.
6	scary	무서운	No, it was scary.
7	hero	영웅	I want to be a hero like him.
8	cook	요리사	I want to be a cook like him.
9	teacher	선생님	I want to be a teacher like him.
10	interesting	흥미로운	It was interesting.
11	very	매우	It was very exciting.
12	same	같은	Same here.

Lesson 6 At the Movie Theater (Step Up 2)

	Vocabulary	Meaning	Sentence
1	excited	신 난, 흥분한	I'm so excited.
2	seats*	좌석(들)	Where are our seats?
3	allowed	허락받은	You're not allowed to take photos here.
4	astronaut*	우주인	I want to be an astronaut like her.
5	screen	화면	Where is the largest IMAX movie screen?
6	wide	폭이 ~인	It is 35.72m wide and 29.57m high.
7	high	높이가 ~인	It is 35.72m wide and 29.57m high.
8	curry	카레	What do you know about India? Curry?
9	every year*	해마다	Over 1,000 films are made every year in India.
10	recognize*	알아보다, 알다	Can you recognize it?
11	red carpet	(시상식의) 레드 카펫	It's a red carpet for the movie première of Harry Potter.
12	première*	개봉	It's the longest red carpet for the movie première.

Lesson 3 Welcome to Hawaii (Step Up 1)

	Vocabulary	Meaning	Sentence
1	long	오랫동안, 긴	Long time no see.
2	check out	확인하다	Check this movie out.
3	watch	보다	Let's watch it.
4	house	집	Let's go to my house first.
5	first	우선, 먼저	Let's go to my house first.
6	lady*	숙녀	Well, let's ask that lady.
7	called	~라고 불리는	Hawaii is called "Aloha State."
8	harmony*	조화	It means kindness and harmony, too.
9	island	섬	Hawaii is called "Big Island."
10	active volcano*	활화산	There is an active volcano, Kilauea.
11	lava*	용암	The lava from the volcano makes new land.
12	rainbow	무지개	Hawaii is called the "Rainbow State."

Lesson 4 Enjoy the Movie

	Vocabulary	Meaning	Sentence
1	bring your pet*	애완견을 데려오다	You're not allowed to bring your pet in here.
2	copy the book*	책을 복사하다	You're not allowed to copy the book in here.
3	eat or drink*	먹거나 마시다	You're not allowed to eat or drink in here.
4	speak loudly*	큰소리로 말하다	You're not allowed to speak loudly in here.
5	feed the animals	동물들에게 먹이를 주다	You're not allowed to feed the animals in here.
6	take pictures	사진을 찍다	You're not allowed to take pictures in here.
7	enjoy	즐기다	Enjoy the movie.
8	play	연극	Enjoy the play.
9	concert	연주회	Enjoy the concert.
10	soda	탄산음료	Let's get some soda and popcorn.
11	fifth	5번째의	Our seats are in the fifth row.
12	row	열, 줄	Our seats are in the fifth row.

Lesson 7 Here Is Your Bag

	Vocabulary	Meaning	Sentence
1	plant the flower*	꽃을 심다	Could you plant the flower?
2	sow the seeds*	씨를 뿌리다	Could you sow the seeds?
3	trim the tree*	나무를 다듬다	Could you trim the tree?
4	water the lawn*	잔디에 물을 주다	Could you water the lawn?
5	mow the lawn	잔디를 깎다	Could you mow the lawn?
6	dig a hole	구멍을 파다	Could you dig a hole?
7	bag	가방	Here is your bag.
8	phone	전화기	Here is your phone.
9	umbrella	우산	Here is your umbrella.
10	get	잡다	Get him!
11	give	주다	Could you give me a ball?
12	here	여기	Here is your bag.

Lesson 8 It's a Little Bit Salty

	Vocabulary	Meaning	Sentence
1	bitter*	쓴	It's a little bit bitter.
2	salty*	짠	It's a little bit salty.
3	sour*	신	It's a little bit sour.
4	spicy*	매운	It's a little bit spicy.
5	greasy	기름진	It's a little bit greasy.
6	sweet	달콤한	It's a little bit sweet.
7	pizza	피자	Can I have another pizza?
8	sandwich	샌드위치	Can I have another sandwich?
9	doughnut	도넛	Can I have another doughnut?
10	smell	~한 냄새가 나다	The pizzas smell good.
11	buy	사다	Let's buy one.
12	taste	맛이 나다	How does it taste?

Lesson 9 At a Hawaiian Restaurant (Step Up 3)

	Vocabulary	Meaning	Sentence
1	friend	친구	This is my **friend**, Tutu.
2	meet	만나다	Nice to **meet** you.
3	hungry	배고픈	I'm **hungry**.
4	restaurant*	식당	This **restaurant** is the best in Hawaii.
5	order	주문	May I take your **order**?
6	special	특별한	Aloha **Special** Fish Set B, please.
7	fish	생선	Hawaiian Special **Fish** Set B, please.
8	enough*	충분히	It's not salty **enough**, but it's okay.
9	pass*	건네주다	Could you **pass** me the salt?
10	cavities*	충치(들)	It helps keep our skin healthy and prevents **cavities**.
11	bones*	뼈(들)	Greek yogurt is a little bit sour, but it is good for your **bones**.
12	health	건강	Gimchi is a litte bit spicy, but it is good for your **health**.

Lesson 11 What's Up?

	Vocabulary	Meaning	Sentence
1	ask for advice*	충고를 구하다	I'm calling to **ask for advice**.
2	ask for help*	도움을 청하다	I'm calling to **ask for help**.
3	say sorry*	미안하다고 말하다	I'm calling to **say sorry**.
4	say thank you*	고맙다고 말하다	I'm calling to **say thank you**.
5	invite you to dinner	저녁 식사에 초대하다	I'm calling to **invite you to dinner**.
6	say goodbye	잘 가라고 말하다	I'm calling to **say goodbye**.
7	peanut	땅콩	Bob loves **peanut** butter.
8	should	~ 해야 한다	You **should** call him.
9	call	전화하다	You should **call** him.
10	speak	말하다	May I **speak** to Bob?
11	lab	연구실	I'm calling to invite you to my **lab**.
12	love	대단히 ~하고 싶다	I'd **love** to go there.

Lesson 14 I Have Something to Show You

	Vocabulary	Meaning	Sentence
1	car accident*	자동차 사고	I'm late because of a **car accident**.
2	flat tire*	바람 빠진 타이어	I'm late because of a **flat tire**.
3	heavy snow*	폭설	I'm late because of the **heavy snow**.
4	roadwork*	도로 공사	I'm late because of the **roadwork**.
5	heavy rain	폭우	I'm late because of the **heavy rain**.
6	traffic jam	교통 체증	I'm late because of a **traffic jam**.
7	show	보여 주다	I have something to **show** you.
8	see	보다	I can't wait to **see** it.
9	tell	말하다	I have something to **tell** you.
10	hear	듣다	I can't wait to **hear** it.
11	give	주다	I have something to **give** you.
12	get	얻다	I can't wait to **get** it.

Lesson 15 My Key Is Missing

	Vocabulary	Meaning	Sentence
1	backpack*	배낭	My **backpack** is missing.
2	cell phone*	휴대 전화	My **cell phone** is missing.
3	key*	열쇠	My **key** is missing.
4	wallet*	지갑	My **wallet** is missing.
5	helmet	헬멧	My **helmet** is missing.
6	necklace	목걸이	My **necklace** is missing.
7	tired	피곤한	I'm so **tired**.
8	surprised	놀라운	I'm so **surprised**.
9	excited	흥분한	I'm so **excited**.
10	invention	발명품	It's my new **invention**.
11	open	열다	**Open** the box.
12	look for	~을 찾다	Let's **look for** it together.

Lesson 12 Can You Take Me to Thomas' Lab?

	Vocabulary	Meaning	Sentence
1	bookstore*	서점	Can you take me to the **bookstore**?
2	opera theater*	오페라 극장	Can you take me to the **opera theater**?
3	post office*	우체국	Can you take me to the **post office**?
4	TV station*	방송국	Can you take me to the **TV station**?
5	airport	공항	Can you take me to the **airport**?
6	hospital	병원	Can you take me to the **hospital**?
7	there	거기(에)	Call me when you get **there**.
8	home	집	Call me when you get **home**.
9	school	학교	Call me when you get to **school**.
10	take	데려가다	Can you **take** me to Thomas' Lab?
11	traffic	교통	The **traffic** is heavy.
12	No problem.	(부탁, 질문에 대해) 그럼요.	**No problem.**

Lesson 13 An Invitation to a Party (Step Up 4)

	Vocabulary	Meaning	Sentence
1	party	파티, 잔치	I'm calling to invite you to my **party**.
2	come	오다	Can you **come**?
3	leave*	떠나다	Let's **leave**.
4	alone*	홀로, 외로이	If you are **alone** on an island what will you do?
5	scared	두려워하는	Don't be **scared**.
6	order	순서	Just do these things in **order**.
7	drink	마시다	Find water you can **drink**.
8	shelter*	피난처	Build a **shelter**.
9	fire	불	Build a **fire**.
10	rescue*	구조	Make a **rescue** signal fire.
11	food	음식	Find some **food** you can eat.
12	wave	흔들다	Then **wave** your arms and jump up and down.

Lesson 16 A Gift for Tutu (Step Up 5)

	Vocabulary	Meaning	Sentence
1	buying	사는 것	How about **buying** a gift for Tutu?
2	gift	선물	How about buying a **gift** for Tutu?
3	flowers	꽃(들)	These **flowers** are beautiful.
4	agree*	동의하다	I **agree**.
5	late	늦은	We're **late**.
6	hurry	서두르다	Let's **hurry**.
7	parking*	주차	The **parking** ticket is missing.
8	because of	~ 때문에	We're late **because of** these flowers.
9	diary	일기장	Tom's **Diary**: Candy Is Missing.
10	run away*	도망가다	Did she **run away**?
11	closet	옷장	Then I went to my room and opened the **closet**.
12	licked*	핥았다	She jumped on me and **licked** my face.

Lesson 17 I Smell Something Greasy

	Vocabulary	Meaning	Sentence
1	hear*	듣다	I **hear** something beeping.
2	beeping*	삑 소리를 내는	I hear something **beeping**.
3	crying*	울부짖는	I hear something **crying**.
4	smell*	냄새를 맡다	I **smell** something burning.
5	burning*	타는	I smell something **burning**.
6	rotten*	썩은	I smell something **rotten**.
7	baking	굽는	I smell something **baking**.
8	breaking	깨지는	I hear something **breaking**.
9	cat	고양이	It's a robot **cat**.
10	doctor	의사	It's a robot **doctor**.
11	teacher	선생님	It's a robot **teacher**.
12	greasy	기름진	I smell something **greasy**.

Lesson 18 What a Surprise!

	Vocabulary	Meaning	Sentence
1	brave*	용감한	I'm sure you're brave.
2	gentle*	온화한, 관대한	I'm sure you're gentle.
3	humorous*	재미있는	I'm sure you're humorous.
4	outgoing*	사교적인	I'm sure you're outgoing.
5	shy	부끄러운	I'm sure you're shy.
6	smart	똑똑한	I'm sure you're smart.
7	sweater	스웨터	I made a sweater for you.
8	dinner	저녁 식사	I made dinner for you.
9	give back	돌려주다	Give the key back to us.
10	made	만들었다	I made Rocat for you.
11	surprise	놀라움	What a surprise!
12	sure	확신하는	I'm sure you're happy now, Rodog.

Lesson 19 A Party at Tutu's House (Step Up 6)

	Vocabulary	Meaning	Sentence
1	welcome	환영하다	Welcome to my house.
2	hold	중단하다	Hold on.
3	outside	야외에	I smell something cooking outside.
4	barbecue	바베큐	We're having a barbecue party.
5	starving*	배고픈	I'm starving.
6	food	음식	Have fun and enjoy the food.
7	dance	춤추다	Let's dance!
8	personality*	성격	Here are three personality types.
9	helpful	도움을 주는	You are the helpful type.
10	warm heart	따뜻한 마음	They have warm hearts.
11	competition*	시합	Do you like competition like sports and games?
12	energetic*	활동적인	They like to move fast and are very energetic.

 Memo

 Memo

Answers

Student Book
Answers

Lesson 1 It's an Action Movie
B. Read, look, and match.
p. 8

1. A: What kind of movie is it?
   B: It's a horror movie.
2. A: What kind of movie is it?
   B: It's an action movie.
3. A: What kind of movie is it?
   B: It's a romantic movie.

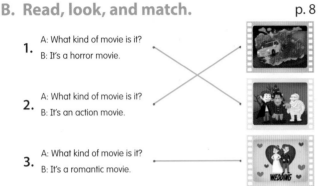

C. Match. Ask and answer.
p. 9

1. fantasy
4. romantic
comedy
5. action
horror
SF
6.

Lesson 2 Let's Help Her
B. Listen, look, and match.
p. 12
1. Blue Street   2. Pink Street   3. Green Street

Lesson 3 Welcome to Hawaii
B. Listen again and write the number in.
p. 14

C. Read and circle True or False.
p. 15
1. False   2. True   3. True   4. False

Reading Time
p. 17
1. It means "Hello" and "Goodbye." It means kindness and harmony, too.
2. It's because people can easily see rainbows.

Lesson 4 Enjoy the Movie
B. Read, look, and match.
p. 20

1. You're not allowed to eat or drink.
2. You're not allowed to copy the book.
3. You're not allowed to bring your pet.
4. You're not allowed to speak loudly.

C. Match and talk.
p. 21

1. the animals   2. or drink   3. loudly
take   feed   bring   eat   copy   speak
4. pictures   5. your pet   6. the book

Lesson 5 It Was Interesting
B. Listen, look, and number.
p. 24
1. 3   2. 1   3. 2   4. 4

Lesson 6 At the Movie Theater
B. Listen again and write the number in.
p. 26

C. Read and circle True or False.   p. 27

1. False   2. False   3. True   4. False

Reading Time   p. 29

1. It's 35.72m wide and 29.57m high.

2. India makes the most movies.

Lesson 7 Here Is Your Bag
B. Look, read, and choose.   p. 32

1. ⓐ   2. ⓑ   3. ⓐ

C. Match. Ask and answer.   p. 33

Lesson 8 It's a Little Bit Salty
B. Listen, look, and check.   p. 36

C. Check. Ask and answer.   p. 37

1. greasy   2. bitter   3. spicy

4. sour   5. salty   6. sweet

Lesson 9 At a Hawaiian Restaurant
B. Listen again and write the number in.
    p. 38

C. Read and circle True or False.   p. 39

1. False   2. False   3. True   4. False

Reading Time   p. 41

1. Greek yogurt is good for our bones.

2. Gimchi has a lot of vitamins

Lesson 10 Assessment Test 1

Listening   p. 42

A. 1. a   2. b   3. a   4. a   5. a   6. b

B. 1. ⓐ   2. ⓑ

Speaking   p. 43

B. ④ Sorry, I didn't know that.

③ You're not allowed to copy the book.

② I'm copying a book.

Reading   p. 44

A. 1. d   2. a   3. f   4. c   5. b   6. e

B. 1. True   2. False   3. True

Writing   p. 45

A. 1. terrible   2. sour

3. stationery store   4. animal clinic

5. sow the seeds   6. speak loudly

7. trim the tree   8. romantic

B. 1. It's a little bit sweet, but it's okay.

2. Yes, it was very exciting.

3. Is there a movie theater near here?

Lesson 11 What's Up?
B. Listen, look, and match.   p. 48

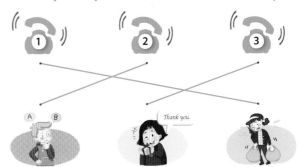

Lesson 12 Can You Take Me to Thomas' Lab?

B. Read, look, and choose. p. 52

1. ⓐ   2. ⓑ   3. ⓐ   4. ⓐ

Lesson 13 An Invitation to a Party

B. Listen again and write the number in.

p. 54

C. Read and circle True or False. p. 55

1. False   2. True   3. True   4. True

Reading Time p. 57

1. Finding water is the most important.

2. I should light a rescue signal fire.

Lesson 14 I Have Something to Show You

B. Look, read, and check. p. 60

1. I'm late because of the roadwork.

2. I'm late because of a flat tire.

3. I'm late because of the heavy rain.

C. Match and talk. p. 61

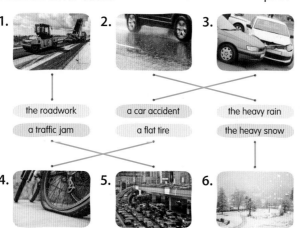

Lesson 15 My Key Is Missing

B. Listen, look, and number. p. 64

C. Match a puzzle and talk. p. 65

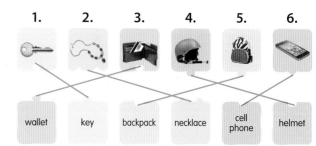

D. Find and color the hidden items. p. 65

Lesson 16 A Gift for Tutu

B. Listen again and write the number in.

p. 66

C. Read and circle True or False.   p. 67

   1. True   **2.** False   **3.** False   **4.** False

Reading Time   p. 69

   1. She called because Candy was missing.

   2. She was in the closet.

Lesson 17 I Smell Something Greasy

B. Look, read, and number.   p. 72

   3   A: I smell something rotten.

   1   A: I smell something burning.

   2   A: I hear something beeping.

C. Match and talk.   p. 73

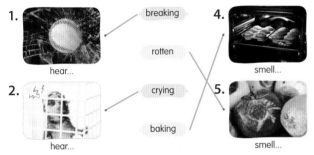

Lesson 18 What a Surprise!

B. Listen, read, and match.   p. 76

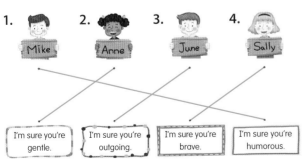

C. Go down the ladder. Then talk.   p. 77

   1. gentle   **2.** brave   **3.** smart

   4. humorous   **5.** outgoing   **6.** shy

Lesson 19 A Party at Tutu's House

B. Listen again and write the number in.

    p. 78

C. Read and circle True or False.   p. 79

   1. True   **2.** True   **3.** False   **4.** True

Reading Time   p. 81

   1. Type **1** people like to meet people.

   2. Type **2** people like to help others.

Lesson 20 Assessment Test 2

Listening   p. 82

A. 1. b   **2.** b   **3.** a   **4.** b   **5.** b   **6.** a

B. 1. ⓑ   **2.** ⓑ

Speaking   p. 83

B. ④ That's okay.

   ② It's me.

   ③ Sorry. I'm late because of the heavy traffic.

Reading   p. 84

A. 1. c   **2.** d   **3.** e   **4.** f   **5.** b   **6.** a

B. 1. ⓐ   **2.** ⓐ   **3.** ⓑ

Writing   p. 85

A. 1. ask for advice   **2.** roadwork

   3. humorous   **4.** rotten

   5. post office   **6.** beeping

   7. backpack   **8.** opera theater

B. 1. I smell something greasy.

   2. Can you take me to Thomas' Lab?

   3. My key is missing.

Workbook
Answers

Lesson 1 It's an Action Movie

A. **2.** action   **3.** romantic   **4.** horror

B. **1.** There's a new movie showing.
   2. What kind of movie is it?

C. **2.** a new musical showing
   3. a new opera showing, Really?

D. **2.** movie is it, horror movie
   3. kind of movie is it, a romantic movie
   4. What kind of movie is it?
      It's an action movie.

Lesson 2 Let's Help Her
pp. 6~7

A. **1.** stationery store   **2.** animal clinic
   3. sports center   **4.** pharmacy

B. **1.** Let's help her.
   2. Yes, there's one on Pine Street.

C. **1.** lost
   2. looks sick, help
   3. looks worried, Let's help him.

D. **2.** a pharmacy near here
   3. there an animal clinic near here
   4. Is there a stationery store near here?
   5. Is there an aquarium near here?
   6. Is there a bus stop near here?

Lesson 3 Welcome to Hawaii
pp. 8~9

A. **1.** action   **2.** romantic   **3.** horror
   4. aquarium   **5.** bus stop   **6.** animal clinic

B. **1.** action
   2. romantic movie
   3. It's a horror movie.
   4. aquarium near here
   5. bus stop near here
   6. Is there an animal clinic near here?

C. **1.** What kind of movie is it?
   2. Where is the bus stop?
   3. Is there a bus stop near here?

Lesson 4 Enjoy the Movie
pp. 10~11

A. **1.** speak loudly
   2. bring your pet
   3. copy the book
   4. eat or drink

B. **1.** Enjoy the movie.
   2. Oh, sorry.

C. **1.** game   **2.** concert, too
   3. Enjoy the play.
      You, too.

D. **2.** speak loudly
   3. allowed to copy the book in here
   4. not allowed to bring your pet in here
   5. You're not allowed to feed the animals in here.
   6. You're not allowed to take pictures in here.

Lesson 5 It Was Interesting
pp. 12~13

A. **1.** fantastic   **2.** touching
   3. boring   **4.** terrible

B. **1.** Did you enjoy the movie?
   2. I want to be a hero like him.

C. **1.** hero
   2. be a cook like him, Same
   3. I want to be a teacher like him.
      Same here.

D. **2.** the movie, was boring
   3. enjoy the movie, it was touching
   4. Did you enjoy the movie?
      No, it was terrible.

Lesson 6 At Movie Theater
pp. 14~15

A. **1.** fantastic   **2.** touching
   3. terrible   **4.** speak loudly
   5. copy the book   **6.** feed the animals

B. 1. fantastic   2. was touching

   3. terrible   4. speak loudly

   5. allowed to copy the book

   6. allowed to feed the animals

C. 1. You're not allowed to take pictures here.

   2. I want to be an astronaut like her.

   3. Yes, it was fantastic.

Lesson 7 Here Is Your Bag   pp. 16~17

A. 1. plant the flower   2. trim the tree

   3. sow the seeds   4. water the lawn

B. 1. Could you give me the ball?

   2. Here is your bag.

C. 1. bag, Thank

   2. is your phone, Thank

   3. is your umbrella, Thank you.

D. 2. water the lawn

   3. you plant the flower

   4. Could you sow the seeds?

   5. Could you dig a hole?

   6. Could you mow the lawn?

Lesson 8 It's a Little Bit Salty   pp. 18~19

A. 1. spicy   2. sour

   3. salty   4. bitter

B. 1. How does it taste?

   2. Can I have another pizza?

C. 1. pizza

   2. have another doughnut, Sure.

   3. Can I have another sandwich?, Sure.

D. 2. taste, bit bitter

   3. does it taste, a little bit spicy

   4. How does it taste?

     It's a little bit greasy.

Lesson 9 At a Hawaiian Restaurant

pp. 20~21

A. 1. spicy   2. sour   3. salty

   4. sow the seeds

   5. trim the tree

   6. dig a hole

B. 1. dig a hole

   2. you trim the tree

   3. Could you sow the seeds?

   4. little bit salty

   5. a little bit sour

   6. It's a little bit spicy.

C. 1. How does it taste?

   2. Could you pass me the salt?

   3. Can I have some more?

Lesson 11 What's Up?   pp. 22~23

A. 1.    2.   3.   4.

ask for help   say sorry   ask for advice   say thank you

B. 1. May I speak to Bob?

   2. What's up?

C. 1. Anne

   2. speak to Mike, Speaking.

   3. May I speak to Sally?, Speaking.

D. 2. ask for help

   3. calling to say sorry

   4. I'm calling to say thank you.

   5. I'm calling to invite you to dinner.

   6. I'm calling to say goodbye.

Lesson 12 Can You Take Me to Thomas' Lab?   pp. 24~25

A. 1. post office   2. TV station

   3. bookstore   4. opera theater

B. 1. Can you take me to Thomas' Lab?

2. Okay, I will.

C. 1. home

2. get to school, I will

3. when you get to the park, I will

D. 2. to the opera theater

3. me to the post office

4. take me to the TV station

5. Can you take me to the airport?

6. Can you take me to the hospital?

Lesson 13 An Invitation to a Party

pp. 26~27

A. 1. airport

2. TV station

3. hospital

4. say goodbye

5. ask for help

6. invite you to dinner

B. 1. ask for help

2. to say goodbye

3. calling to invite you to dinner

4. to the TV station

5. take me to the airport

6. Can you take me to the hospital?

C. 1. I'm calling to invite you to my party.

2. Can you take me to Tutu's house?

3. I'm so excited.

Lesson 14 I Have Something to Show You

pp. 28~29

A. 1.   2.   3.   4.

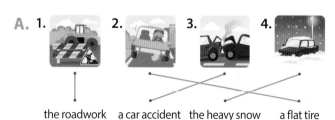

the roadwork   a car accident   the heavy snow   a flat tire

B. 1. That's okay.

2. I can't wait to see it.

C. 1. show, see

2. to tell you, hear it

3. something to give you, get it

D. 2. because of the heavy snow

3. late because of the roadwork

4. I'm late because of a flat tire.

5. I'm late because of a traffic jam.

6. I'm late because of the heavy rain.

Lesson 15 My Key Is Missing

pp. 30~31

A. 1. cell phone   2. wallet

3. key   4. backpack

B. 1. I'm so excited.

2. Let's look for it together.

C. 1. excited

2. tired, too

3. surprised

Me, too.

D. 2. wallet, it together

3. My backpack is, look for it together

4. My necklace is missing.

Let's look for it together.

Lesson 16 A Gift for Tutu

pp. 32~33

A. 1. backpack   2. key

3. cell phone   4. a car accident

5. the roadwork   6. the heavy snow

B. 1. of the roadwork

2. because of a car accident

3. late because of the heavy snow

4. My backpack is

5. cell phone is missing

6. My key is missing.

C. 1. Let's hurry.

2. Let's look for it together.

3. We're late because of these flowers.

Lesson 17 I Smell Something Greasy

pp. 34~35

A.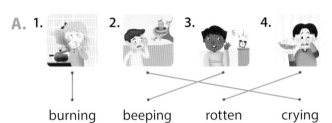

1. burning
2. beeping (2→crying)
3. rotten (3→beeping)
4. crying (4→rotten)

burning   beeping   rotten   crying

B. 1. So do I.
   2. What's your new invention?

C. 1. robot cat
   2. new invention, robot teacher
   3. new invention, robot doctor

D. 2. smell, rotten
   3. I smell something baking.
   4. hear, crying
   5. hear, beeping
   6. I hear something breaking.

Lesson 18 What a Surprise!

pp. 36~37

A. 1. outgoing   2. brave
   3. humorous   4. gentle

B. 1. I made Rocat for you.
   2. I'm sure you're happy.

C. 1. a doll
   2. a sweater for you, surprise
   3. dinner for you, surprise

D. 2. you're gentle
   3. sure you're brave
   4. I'm sure you're humorous.
   5. I'm sure you're shy.
   6. I'm sure you're smart.

Lesson 19 A Party at Tutu's House

pp. 38~39

A. 1. smart   2. outgoing   3. shy
   4. beeping   5. rotten   6. burning

B. 1. smart   2. outgoing   3. shy
   4. beeping   5. rotten
   6. something burning

C. 1. I smell something cooking outside.
   2. I'm sure you're hungry.
   3. Have fun and enjoy the food.

Final Test
English Town Book 6

1. ③	2. ④	3. ⑤	4. ②	5. ④
6. ④	7. ⑤	8. ①	9. ②	10. ①
11. ③	12. ④	13. ⑤	14. ③	15. ⑤
16. ③	17. hear	18. sure		

19. because of the roadwork

20. You're not allowed to speak loudly

Memo

Final Test_English Town Book 6

[13-14] Read and answer the questions.

Bob: Thank you _____ coming to my birthday party.

Stella: Happy birthday, Bob. This cake is for you.

Bob: What a surprise! Thank you.

13 **What is the right one for the blank?**

① of ② in ③ to
④ on ⑤ for

14 **What is Stella's present for Bob?**

① car ② card ③ cake
④ robot ⑤ party

16 **Which place is Mandy looking for?**

① bank ② hospital
③ pharmacy ④ post office
⑤ opera theater

[17-18] Choose and write the right word.

smell   hear   sure   okay

17

A: I _____ something beeping.

B: So do I.

Final Test
English Town Book 6

Class	Name	Score
		/20

Part 1 - Listening

[1-2] Listen and choose the right expression.

1

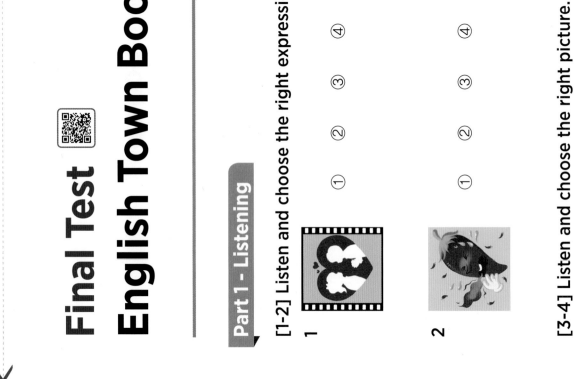

① ② ③ ④ ⑤

2

① ② ③ ④ ⑤

[3-4] Listen and choose the right picture.

3 ① ② ③

Part 2 - Speaking

[7-8] Listen and choose the best response.

7 ① It's me.
② Thank you.
③ This is Amy.
④ Sorry, I didn't know that.
⑤ I'm calling to say thank you.

8 ① Same here. ② No problem.
③ It was scary. ④ It was boring.
⑤ Let's help her.

9 Listen and choose the wrong conversation.

① ② ③ ④ ⑤

① ② ③ ④ ⑤

Part 3 - Reading

[11-12] Choose the right one for the blank.

11

A: _____ kind of movie is it?

B: It's an action movie.

① How   ② Who   ③ What

④ Which   ⑤ Where

12

A: _____

B: Okay. Here you are.

① What's up?

② Who's there?

③ Did you enjoy the musical?

④ Could you give me the ball?

⑤ Can you take me to the airport?

4

①   ②   ③

④   ⑤

[5-6] Listen and choose the right conversation.

5

①   ②   ③   ④   ⑤

6

①   ②   ③   ④   ⑤

[15-16] Read and answer the questions.

Mandy: Excuse me. Can I ask a question?

Man: Sure. Go ahead.

Mandy: Is there a pharmacy near here?

Man: _____

Walk up this street and turn left. It's
next to the hospital.

Mandy: Thank you.

15 What is the right one for the blank?

① I don't know.

② No, there isn't.

③ Where is the pharmacy?

④ There is a hospital near here.

⑤ Yes, there's one on Park Street.

18

A: I'm _____ you're brave.

B: Yes, I am.

[19-20] Unscramble and write.

19 A: I'm late

_____ .

(of / because / roadwork / the)

B: That's okay.

20 A: _____ in here.

(not / to / allowed / You're / loudly / speak)

B: Oh, sorry.

ENGLISH TOWN

FOR EVERYONE

BOOK

6

WORKBOOK

YBM

ENGLISH TOWN

TOWN

FOR
EVERYONE

BOOK

6

WORKBOOK

Contents

It's an Action Movie

A. Look, check, and write twice.

①

☑ SF
☐ horror

<u>SF</u>
<u>SF</u>

②

☐ SF
☐ action

_____
_____

③

☐ fantasy
☐ romantic

_____
_____

④

☐ horror
☐ romantic

_____
_____

B. Choose and write the sentence.

> There's a new movie showing.

> What kind of movie is it?

①

A _____

B Really?

②

A _____

B It's an action movie.

C. Look and write.

①

movie

A There's a new _____movie_____ showing.

B Really?

②

musical

A There's _____.

B Really?

③

opera

A There's _____.

B _____

D. Complete the dialogs using the given word.

1. (SF)   **A** What kind of movie is it?

   B It's an _____SF_____ movie.

2. (horror)   **A** What kind of _____?

   B It's a _____.

3. (romantic)   **A** What _____?

   B It's _____.

4. (action)   **A** _____

   B _____

Let's Help Her

animal clinic   pharmacy
stationery store   sports center

A. Choose and write twice.

_____

_____

_____

_____

_____

_____

_____

_____

B. Choose and write the sentence.

| Yes, there's one on Pine Street. | Let's help her. |

A That girl looks lost.

B _____

A Is there a movie theater near here?

B _____

C. Look and write.

①

lost

A That girl looks _____ .

B Let's help her.

②

sick

A That man _____ .

B Let's _____ him.

③

worried

A That man _____ .

B _____

D. Complete the questions using the given words.

1. (sports center)   Is there a ___sports center___ near here?

2. (pharmacy)   Is there _____ ?

3. (animal clinic)   Is _____ ?

4. (stationery store)   _____

5. (aquarium)   _____

6. (bus stop)   _____

Lesson 3 — Welcome to Hawaii

| romantic | action | horror |
| animal clinic | aquarium | bus stop |

A. Choose and write.

①

_____

②

_____

③

_____

④

_____

⑤

_____

⑥

_____

B. Complete the sentences using the words in A.

1. It's an _____ movie. I'm crazy about action movies.

2. It's a _____ I'm crazy about romantic movies.

3. _____ I'm crazy about horror movies.

4. I want to see a dolphin. Is there an _____ ?

5. I have to take a bus. Is there a _____ ?

6. My dog is sick. _____

8

C. Can you remember the story? Choose and write.

> Where is the bus stop?

> What kind of movie is it?

> Is there a bus stop near here?

A _____

B It's an SF movie.

A _____

B Well... let's ask that lady.

A Excuse me. _____

B Yes, there's one on River Road.

Reading Time Read and write.

island

lava

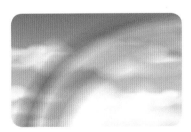

rainbow

_____

_____

Lesson 4

Enjoy the Movie

bring your pet   eat or drink
speak loudly   copy the book

 A. Choose and write twice.

①
_____

_____

②
_____

_____

③
_____

_____

④
_____

_____

B. Choose and write the sentence.

Enjoy the movie.   Oh, sorry.

①

A _____

B You, too.

②

A You're not allowed to take pictures in here.

B _____

10

C. Look and write.

①

game

A Enjoy the _____ .

B You, too.

②

concert

A Enjoy the _____ .

B You, _____ .

③

play

A _____

B _____

D. Complete the sentences using the given words.

1. (eat or drink)   You're not allowed to ___eat or drink___ in here.

2. (speak loudly)   You're not allowed to _____ in here.

3. (copy the book)   You're not _____ .

4. (bring your pet) You're _____ .

5. (feed the animals) _____

6. (take pictures)   _____

It Was Interesting

A. Look, check, and write twice.

①
- ☐ sad
- ☐ fantastic

_____
_____

②
- ☐ sleepy
- ☐ touching

_____
_____

③
- ☐ boring
- ☐ excited

_____
_____

④
- ☐ terrible
- ☐ happy

_____
_____

B. Choose and write the sentence.

| I want to be a hero like him. | Did you enjoy the movie? |

①

A _____

B Yes, it was very exciting.

②

A _____

B Same here.

C. Look and write.

1

hero

A I want to be a _____ like him.

B Same here.

2

cook

A I want to _____.

B _____ here.

3

teacher

A _____

B _____

D. Complete the dialogs using the given word.

1. (fantastic)   **A** Did you enjoy the movie?

                    B Yes, it was ____fantastic____.

2. (boring)   **A** Did you enjoy _____?

                  B No, it _____.

3. (touching)   **A** Did you _____?

                   B Yes, _____.

4. (terrible)   **A** _____

                  B _____

At Movie Theater

| terrible | touching | fantastic |
| feed the animals | speak loudly | copy the book |

A. Choose and write.

①

②

③

④

⑤

⑥

B. Complete the sentences using the words in A.

1. I enjoyed the party. It was _____.

2. I cried because the movie _____.

3. The food was _____. I'm hungry now.

4. You're not allowed to _____ in the museum.

5. You're not _____ in the library.

6. You're not _____ in the zoo.

C. Can you remember the story? Unscramble the words.

A _____
(not / here / allowed to / You're / take / pictures / .)

B Sorry, I didn't know that.

A _____
(want / to / an / astronaut / I / be / like / her / .)

B Same here.

A Did you enjoy the movie?

B _____
(fantastic / Yes, / it / was / .)

Reading Time Read and write.

screen

curry

red carpet

_____   _____   _____

_____   _____   _____

Lesson 7

Here Is Your Bag

A. Choose and write twice.

> trim the tree   sow the seeds
> water the lawn   plant the flower

_____
_____

_____
_____

_____
_____

_____
_____

B. Choose and write the sentence.

> Could you give me the ball?   Here is your bag.

A _____

B Okay.

A _____

B Thank you.

C. Look and write.

①
bag

A Here is your _____ .

B _____ you.

②
phone

A Here _____ .

B _____ you.

③
umbrella

A Here _____ .

B _____

D. Complete the questions using the given words.

1. (trim the tree) Could you _____ trim the tree _____ ?

2. (water the lawn) Could you _____ ?

3. (plant the flower) Could _____ ?

4. (sow the seeds) _____

5. (dig a hole) _____

6. (mow the lawn) _____

It's a Little Bit Salty

A. Look, check, and write twice.

1
- [ ] spicy
- [ ] sweet

_____

_____

2
- [ ] sour
- [ ] greasy

_____

_____

3
- [ ] hot
- [ ] salty

_____

_____

4
- [ ] bitter
- [ ] sweet

_____

_____

B. Choose and write the sentence.

Can I have another pizza?	How does it taste?

1

A _____

B It's a little bit salty, but it's okay.

2

A _____

B Sure. You eat a lot.

C. Look and write.

1

pizza

A Can I have another _____ ?

B Sure.

2

doughnut

A Can I _____ ?

B _____

3

sandwich

A _____

B _____

D. Complete the dialogs using the given word.

1. (sour)
   A How does it taste?

   B It's a little bit ____sour____ .

2. (bitter)
   A How does it _____ ?

   B It's a little _____ .

3. (spicy)
   A How _____ ?

   B It's _____ .

4. (greasy)
   A _____

   B _____

Lesson 9

At a Hawaiian Restaurant

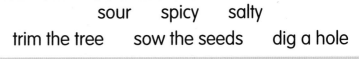

sour   spicy   salty

trim the tree   sow the seeds   dig a hole

A. Choose and write.

① _____

② _____

③ _____

④ _____

⑤ _____

⑥ _____

B. Unscramble the words.

1. Could you _____ ?
   (a hole / dig)

2. Could _____ ?
   (the tree / you / trim)

3. _____
   (the seeds / Could / you / sow / ?)

4. It's a _____ .
   (salty / little / bit)

5. It's _____ .
   (a little / sour / bit)

6. _____
   (spicy / It's / a little / bit / .)

C. **Can you remember the story? Choose and write.**

> Can I have some more?   Could you pass me the salt?

> How does it taste?

A _____

B It's not salty enough, but it's okay.

A _____

B Sure. Here you are.

A _____

B Sure.

Reading Time   **Read and write.**

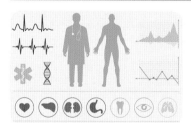

health

cavity

bone

_____   _____   _____

_____   _____   _____

Lesson **11**

What's Up?

A. Look, match, and write twice.

①

②

③

④

ask for help   say sorry   ask for advice   say thank you

_____   _____   _____   _____

_____   _____   _____   _____

B. Choose and write the sentence.

| May I speak to Bob? | What's up? |

①

A _____

B Speaking.

②

A _____

B I'm calling to invite you to my lab.

C. Look and write.

1

  A May I speak to _____?

  B Speaking.

2

  A May I _____?

  B _____

3

  A _____

  B _____

D. Complete the sentences using the given words.

1. (ask for advice)   I'm calling to _____ask for advice_____ .

2. (ask for help)   I'm calling to _____ .

3. (say sorry)   I'm _____ .

4. (say thank you)   _____

5. (invite you to dinner)   _____

6. (say goodbye)   _____

Can You Take Me to Thomas' Lab?

A. Look, check, and write twice.

1
- ☐ hospital
- ☐ post office

_____

_____

2
- ☐ TV station
- ☐ museum

_____

_____

3
- ☐ aquarium
- ☐ bookstore

_____

_____

4
- ☐ opera theater
- ☐ movie theater

_____

_____

B. Choose and write the sentence.

| Okay, I will. | Can you take me to Thomas' Lab? |

1

A _____

B Sure.

2

A Call me when you get there.

B _____

C. Look and write.

1
home

A Call me when you get _____ .

B Okay, I will.

2
to school

A Call me when you _____ .

B Okay, _____ .

3
to the park

A Call me _____ .

B Okay, _____ .

D. Complete the questions using the given words.

1. (bookstore)   Can you take me to the ___bookstore___ ?

2. (opera theater)   Can you take me _____ ?

3. (post office)   Can you take _____ ?

4. (TV station)   Can you _____ ?

5. (airport)   _____

6. (hospital)   _____

Lesson 13

An Invitation to a Party

Step Up 4

| airport | hospital | TV station | say goodbye |
| invite you to dinner | ask for help |

A. Choose and write.

①  ②  ③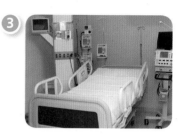

_____ _____ _____

④  ⑤  ⑥

_____ _____ _____

B. Unscramble the words.

1. I'm calling to _____ .
   (help / ask / for)

2. I'm calling _____ .
   (say / to / goodbye)

3. I'm _____ .
   (to / you / to dinner / invite / calling)

4. Can you take me _____ ?
   (TV station / the / to)

5. Can you _____ ?
   (to / airport / the / me / take)

6. _____
   (take / to / me / the / Can / you / hospital / ?)

26

C. Can you remember the story? Choose and write.

I'm so excited.

I'm calling to invite you to my party.

Can you take me to Tutu's house?

A What's up?

B _____

A _____

B Sure. She invited me, too.

A Let's leave.

B Okay. _____

Reading Time Read and write.

scared

shelter

rescue

_____

_____

_____

_____

_____

_____

I Have Something to Show You

A. Look, match, and write twice.

①

②

③

④

the roadwork

a car accident

the heavy snow

a flat tire

_____

_____

_____

_____

B. Choose and write the sentence.

I can't wait to see it.

That's okay.

①

A I'm late because of the heavy traffic.

B _____

②

A I have something to show you.

B _____

C. Look and write.

show / see

A I have something to _____ you.

B I can't wait to _____ it.

tell / hear

A I have something _____.

B I can't wait to _____.

give / get

A I have _____.

B I can't wait to _____.

D. Complete the sentences using the given words.

1. (a car accident) I'm late because of ___a car accident___.

2. (the heavy snow) I'm late _____.

3. (the roadwork) I'm _____.

4. (a flat tire) _____.

5. (a traffic jam) _____.

6. (the heavy rain) _____

Lesson 15

My Key Is Missing

A. Look, check, and write twice.

1
- [ ] computer
- [ ] cell phone

_____
_____

2
- [ ] wallet
- [ ] notebook

_____
_____

3
- [ ] key
- [ ] spoon

_____
_____

4
- [ ] backpack
- [ ] lunch box

_____
_____

B. Choose and write the sentence.

I'm so excited.   Let's look for it together.

1

A What is it? _____

B Me, too.

2

A My key is missing.

B Really? _____

C. Look and write.

①
excited

A I'm so _____.

B Me, too.

②
tired

A I'm so _____.

B Me, _____.

③
surprised

A I'm so _____.

B _____.

D. Complete the dialogs using the given word.

1. (key)   A My _____*key*_____ is missing.

             B Let's look for it together.

2. (wallet)   A My _____ is missing.

             B Let's look for _____.

3. (backpack) A _____ missing.

             B Let's _____.

4. (necklace) A _____

             B _____

Lesson 16

A Gift for Tutu

| key | backpack | cell phone |
| the heavy snow | a car accident | the roadwork |

A. Choose and write.

① _____

② _____

③ _____

④ _____

⑤ _____

⑥ _____

B. Unscramble the words.

1. I'm late because _____.
   (of / roadwork / the)

2. I'm late _____.
   (car accident / a / of / because)

3. I'm _____.
   (late / of / because / heavy / snow / the)

4. _____ missing.
   (is / My / backpack)

5. My _____.
   (is / cell phone / missing)

6. _____
   (missing / is / My / key /.)

C. Can you remember the story? Choose and write.

> Let's look for it together.

> We're late because of these flowers.

> Let's hurry.

A We're late. _____

A The parking ticket is missing.

B _____

A _____

B That's okay. How beautiful!

Reading Time

Read and write.

diary

closet

licked

_____

_____

_____

_____

_____

_____

I Smell Something Greasy

A. Look, match, and write twice.

①

②

③

④

burning

beeping

rotten

crying

_____

_____

_____

_____

B. Choose and write the sentence.

What's your new invention?   So do I.

①

A   I smell something greasy.

B   _____

②

A   _____

B   It's a robot cat.

34

C. Look and write.

1

robot cat

A What's your new invention?

B It's a _____.

2

robot teacher

A What's your _____?

B It's a _____.

3

robot doctor

A What's your _____?

B It's a _____.

D. Complete the sentences using the given words.

1. (smell / burning)   I ___smell___ something ___burning___ .

2. (smell / rotten)   I _____ something _____ .

3. (smell / baking)   _____

4. (hear / crying)   I _____ something _____ .

5. (hear / beeping)   I _____ something _____ .

6. (hear / breaking)   _____

What a Surprise!

A. Check and write.

1
☐ funny
☐ outgoing
_____

2
☐ timid
☐ brave
_____

3
☐ shy
☐ humorous
_____

4
☐ gentle
☐ stubborn
_____

B. Choose and write the sentence.

┌─────────────────────────┐   ┌─────────────────────────┐
│ I made Rocat for you.   │   │ I'm sure you're happy. │
└─────────────────────────┘   └─────────────────────────┘

1

A _____

B What a surprise!

2

A _____

B Yes, I am.

C. Look and write.

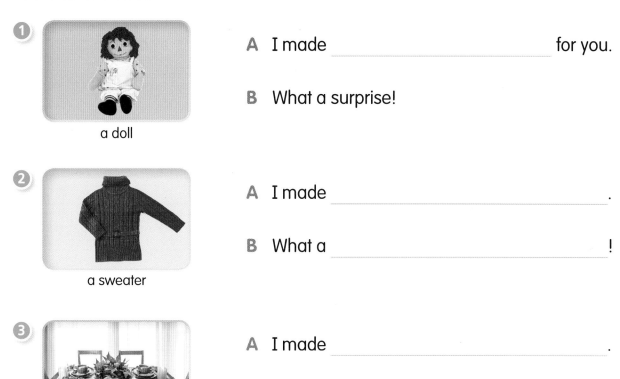

1

a doll

A I made _____ for you.

B What a surprise!

2

a sweater

A I made _____ .

B What a _____ !

3

dinner

A I made _____ .

B What a _____ !

D. Complete the sentences using the given word.

1. (outgoing)   I'm sure you're _____ outgoing _____ .

2. (gentle)   I'm sure _____ .

3. (brave)   I'm _____ .

4. (humorous) _____

5. (shy) _____

6. (smart) _____

Lesson **19**

A Party at Tutu's House

Step Up 6

shy	outgoing	smart
rotten	beeping	burning

A. Choose and write.

①

②

③

_____

_____

_____

④

⑤

⑥

_____

_____

_____

B. Look at A. Complete the sentences.

1. I'm sure he's _____.

2. I'm sure they're _____.

3. I'm sure she's _____.

4. I hear something _____ in the street.

5. I smell something _____ in the fruit box.

6. I smell _____ in the kitchen.

38

C. Can you remember the story? Unscramble the words.

1

A _____
  (smell / I / cooking / outside / something / .)

B We're having a barbecue party.

2

A _____
  (you're / sure / I'm / hungry / .)

B Yes, I am. I'm starving.

3

A _____
  (enjoy / fun / and / Have / the / food / .)

B Thank you.

Reading Time Read and write.

warm heart

competition

energetic

_____ _____ _____

_____ _____ _____

Memo